Austrian Cookbook

Tastes of Vienna and much more

Lukas Procházka

License Note

About the Author

I consider myself to be very skilled cook and a good author of many cookbooks, which are now being sold worldwide. I was born in a small town in the north of Czechia. Since very young age I have been drawn to cooking. In 2012 I wrote my first cookbook about Czech cuisine. Since then I have kept on writing new titles. I hope you find my books to be useful and you will get inspiration from these.

For more cookbooks please visit
www.amazon.com/author/prochazkacook

Subscribe on Twitter to stay informed:
www.twitter.com/ProchazkaCook

CONTENTS

Desserts

Side Dishes

About Austria

Austria's cuisine is characterized by its historic influences. A true melting pot of flavors. Over the hundreds of years of Austria's existence, a unique tradition of Austrian Cuisine has emerged. Its traditional and well-known recipes attract millions of tourists each year. Austria's rich Cuisine is a result of its history as a multi-national empire, where all kinds of different cultures contributed their very own nuances. The Habsburg Empire stretched from the borders of Imperial Russia to the Adriatic and consisted of more than a dozen nationalities with over 51 million people speaking sixteen different languages. Within the last seven centuries, the cosmopolitan Habsburg rule extended over Switzerland, Alsace, Burgundy, Spain, Holland, Bohemia, Moravia, Slovakia, Poland, Hungary, Croatia, Slovenia and Italy. All of the above have influenced Austria's cuisine in their own way.

But not all of what can be enjoyed at Austria's restaurants and cafés nowadays has peacefully found its way into Austria's kitchens. Many a recipe and ingredient had been washed ashore by Austria's melting pot of pan-European cooking by accident or as a coincidence or war. The Turkish invasion of Europe for example heralded the birth of Austria's coffee culture by introducing the coffee bean to Viennese cooks. Furthermore, "Apfelstrudel" is an Austrian version of a Turkish delicacy introduced during the Turkish occupation. The Wiener Schnitzel probably originated in northern Italy, while the delicious Palatschinken and the Goulash came from the Hungarian plains; the roasts and sausages were originally Southern German delicacies, the pastries originated in Bohemia.

Most people refer to Austrian cuisine as Viennese cuisine. This reference is clearly inaccurate. Vienna has been the capital of Austria for more than a thousand years. It became the cultural center of the nation and developed its own regional cuisine, yet it hardly includes more than just a frame of whole Austrian culture.

Appetizers

Powidl, Plum Jam

Chicken Salad

Ingredients:

4 chicken breasts
2 eggs
Flour and breadcrumbs
Butter
Salad
Fresh salad leaves
2 tbsps Styrian balsamic apple vinegar
5 tbsps Styrian pumpkin seed oil
A splash of strong, slightly warmed vegetable stock
A pinch of hot mustard
Cherry tomatoes for the garnish
Salt
Pepper

Directions:

1. Cut the breast into smaller, bite-sized pieces. Season well all over with salt and leave to stand, covered, for around 1 hour
2. Meanwhile, for the marinade stir the mustard into a little of the slightly warmed stock until smooth, and then mix in the vinegar. Season with salt and pepper and mix together with the pumpkin seed oil. Sample it to check the taste. Clean and wash the salad leaves and leave them to drip dry or use a salad spinner.
3. Beat the eggs briefly on a plate or in a bowl, with the flour and breadcrumbs ready on two more plates. Now roll the chicken pieces in the flour to coat them, dip them in the beaten egg and coat them with breadcrumbs.
4. In a pan, heat a good quantity of butter. Place the chicken pieces into the hot fat and, depending on size, cook for 3-7 minutes until golden brown, turning once. Remove and allow to drain on kitchen paper.
5. Meanwhile, marinade the dried salad leaves and arrange them in the centre of large serving plates.
6. Place the crispy chicken pieces on the salad only immediately prior to serving. Garnish with halved cherry tomatoes.

Liptauer, Cheese Spread

Ingredients:

180g cream cheese, softened
2 tbsps sour cream
2 tbsps finely chopped cornichons
2 tbsps finely chopped flat-leaf parsley
2 tbsps snipped chives
1 tsp Dijon mustard
1 1/2 tsp sweet Hungarian paprika
1 teaspoon chopped drained capers
Salt and freshly ground pepper

Directions:

1. In a bowl, mix all of the ingredients until blended.
2. Serve with fresh bread.

Powidl, Plum Spread

Ingredients:

2kg Italian plums
10 cloves
1 cinnamon stick

Directions:

1. Wash the plums and cut them into small pieces (1/2 inch or so), removing the stone as you do it. Place them in a heavy pan and pour a little water in the bottom, no more than a half a cup.
2. Bring the plums to a boil, stirring often so that they don't burn on the bottom. Add the cinnamon stick and the cloves.
3. Boil gently for 3 or more hours, stirring often.
4. Place the cooked plums in a ricer or sieve and stir to remove the skins and spices. Bring the jam back to a boil until it has reduced as far as you want it and is very thick.
5. Ladle the butter into clean, boiled, preserving jars or into freezer bags. Freeze or can, as you wish.

Soups

Speckknödel Soup

Cauliflower Soup

Yield: 6 servings

Ingredients:

1 head cauliflower, chopped
3 large carrots, chopped
1 cup celery, chopped
2 leeks, chopped
4 cloves garlic, minced
2 tablespoons no-salt seasoning
2 cups carrot juice
4 cups water
1 tsp nutmeg
5 cups kale, stems removed and chopped
1 cup raw cashews

Directions:

1. In a large soup pot over high heat, add all ingredients except cashews and kale.
2. Bring to boil, cover and reduce the heat to medium low to simmer for 15 minutes or until vegetables are just tender.
3. Add the kale and cook for 5 minutes or until wilted.
4. In a high-speed blender, add cashews and half the soup. Blend until smooth. Add back to the soup.
5. Serve.

Dumpling Soup

Yield: 8 servings

Ingredients:

5 ½ tbsp unsalted butter
2 eggs, lightly beaten)
⅔ cups white semolina
¼ tsp fine salt
⅛ tsp ground nutmeg
1 tbsp chopped flat parsley
4 cups beef broth
Chopped chives to garnish

Directions:

1. Beat softened butter with an electric hand mixer until creamy, about 1 minute.
2. Gradually add half of the beaten eggs, then half of the semolina. Add the remaining eggs, semolina, nutmeg, salt and parsley and mix until well combined. The mixture should be soft and creamy.
3. Put the batter into the fridge and let it rest for 15 minutes, so it gets firm.
4. Bring a wide pot of generously salted water to a boil. Reduce temperature to medium-low. The water should simmer gently but not be boiling or the dumplings will fall apart.
5. Dip two tablespoons (to avoid sticking) into hot water and form tight, oval quenelles with the aid of 2 tablespoons, so they end up with three clear edges and a smooth surface. If this is too difficult, you can wet your hands and shape them. The important thing is that they need to be really tightly shaped. Don't make them too big, as they will double in bulk.
6. Drop the formed dumplings into the simmering water. If you are using a rather small pot, don't overcrowd it, because the dumplings will plump up.
7. Cook the dumplings in barely simmering water for 5 minutes. Reduce temperature to the lowest possible and let them steep for another 10-15 minutes. By now, they should have doubled in volume. Try one dumpling, if it is still quiet firm in the center, let them steep for a couple more minutes. The dumplings should be soft but not mushy.
8. Meanwhile heat the stock. When the dumplings are done, transfer them with a slotted spoon into soup bowl. Add a ladle of stock and serve sprinkled with chopped chive.

Garlic Soup

Yield: 2 servings

Ingredients:

10 big cloves of garlic, peeled and pushed through a garlic press
¼ cup flour
¾ cup milk
3 tablespoons butter
1½ cup chicken stock
2 tablespoons chopped parsley
½ teaspoon salt
¼ teaspoon pepper
Croutons:
2 slices of white bread, cubed
¼ teaspoons salt
1 tablespoon olive oil

Directions:

1. Preheat the oven to 160.
2. Spread the croutons on a parchment lined baking tray, drizzle with olive oil, sprinkle with salt and toss. Bake for about 5-7 minutes until croutons are slightly browned.
3. Meanwhile, melt the butter in a large sauce pan and on a medium heat. Throw in garlic and stirring constantly, allow it to release all its flavor, about 3-5 minutes. Don't let it get brown.
4. Whisk in flour until it forms a thick paste.
5. Whisking constantly, start incorporating milk ¼ cup at a time. When all milk has been added, pour in chicken stock. Season with salt and pepper and whisk until the soup has thickened and bubbly.
6. Divide the soup between 2 bowls. Sprinkle with a parsley and garnish with croutons.
7. Serve.

Quick Mushroom Soup

Yield: 6 servings

Ingredients:

4 cups beef stock
1 cup thinly sliced mushroom
4 tbsps butter
4 tsp dry sherry
2 tablespoons chopped chives

Directions:

1. In a large saucepan, combine stock and mushrooms, bring to a boil.
2. Add butter if using canned broth and simmer 2 minutes.
3. Remove from heat and stir in sherry.
4. Ladle into soup bowls and top with chives.

Rindsuppe, Austrian Beef Soup

Yield: 8 servings

Ingredients:

600g beef bones and a piece of beef chuck
Carrots
Celery root
Leeks
Parsley root
Garlic
2 whole unskinned onions
5 pepper corns
2 juniper berries
2 bay leaves
Salt

Directions:

1. Bring water to a boil and place bones in the boiling water. After boiling a minute or two, drain bones in colander and rinse with cold water. Now placing the bones in your soup pot, fill with fresh cold water and bring to a boil.
2. From now on, the broth should not cook too strongly, rather simmer. If the broth boils, it will not stay clear but will become muddy. Add a piece of beef, which not only adds flavor to your soup, but also is nice when chopped and served later with the broth.
3. Especially at the beginning, a lot of grey scum will rise to the surface skim it off frequently. As the cooking proceeds, less and less scum appears.
4. After about an hour cut the onions in half and sear them on the cut surface 'til it blackens. You can do this either directly on the stovetop or in a pan. Add the onions, root vegetables, herbs, but not the salt--only add salt when the broth is ready. The broth acquires a nice golden color from the onion skins.
5. When that piece of meat is tender, the broth is golden, has a strong good aroma and the vegetables are cooked, it is ready to serve. Season with salt and maybe more ground pepper. Chop and add some of the vegetables and the meat and sprinkle with freshly chopped chives or another chopped herb.

Speckknoedel Soup

Yield: 6 servings

Ingredients:

300g of stale bread rolls
100g of smoked bacon (Speck)
1/2 onion
10g butter, melted
3 eggs
1/4 l milk
4 tbsp chopped parsley
2 tbsp flour
Salt to season
6 cups of beef broth

Directions:

1. Cut the bread rolls into cubes approximately 1/2 inch wide, and place in a bowl. Cube the bacon small and sauté over medium heat until it starts to go translucent. Peel and chop the onion finely, sauté with the bacon until the onions too become translucent.
2. Add the two spoonfuls of parsley, continue to sauté.
3. Add the sautéed mixture to the cubed bread. Beat the eggs and milk together: add to the bread mixture with the rest of the parsley. Sprinkle in the flour and add the butter, season with salt and pepper, and mix well to blend all the ingredients. Allow to rest for 30 minutes.
4. Bring to a boil at least three liters of salted water. Reduce to a simmer. With your hands, form the dumpling mixture into six balls. Add gently to the boiling water and cook for approximately fifteen minutes.
5. Pour hot broth in bowls and add dumplings. Serve.

Viennese Potato Soup

Yield: 4 servings

Ingredients:

200g potatoes
1 onion
50g breakfast bacon
100g carrots and celery
4 tbsps vegetable oil
20g flour
1 1/4 l beef broth
1 tbsp caraway seeds
1 clove garlic
1 tbsp parsley
1 tbsp celery leaves (chopped)
1 leaf bay
10g edible boletus
1 tbsp Apple vinegar
2 tbsp Sour cream
Salt
Pepper
Marjoram

Directions:

1. Soak boletus in warm water.
2. Dice the potatoes, cut onion, bacon, carrots and celery into small cubes.
3. Heat oil in a large pot; fry the onion, bacon, carrots and celery slowly until translucent.
4. Add the flour, sauté lightly, add beef broth, and blend until smooth. Season with salt, pepper, marjoram, caraway seed, crushed garlic, chopped parsley, celery leaves and bay leaf.
5. Remove boletus from the soaking liquid, chop coarsely, and add to the soup. Strain mushroom soaking liquid through a kitchen cloth and add to the soup.
6. Cook for approximately 15 minutes, then add the potatoes and cook until they are soft.
7. Stir in the sour cream, remove from the hot plate and season with salt, pepper and vinegar.

Main Courses

Käsespätzle

Beuschel

Yield: 4 servings

Ingredients:

600g veal lungs
1 veal heart
1 root vegetables (parsley, carrots, celery stalk)
6 peppercorns
3 allspice corns
1 bay leaf
1 sprig thyme
1 onion
40g butter
30 flour
1 cooking spoon capers
1 onion, halved
1 anchovy fillet, chopped
1 clove garlic, minced
Lemon rind, grated
1 tbsp parsley, chopped
Dash of vinegar
Sugar
Pinch of ground marjoram
Smidgen of mustard
2 tbsps sour cream
2 tbsps cream
Dash of lemon juice
4 tbsps goulash sauce
Pepper
Salt

Directions:

1. Separate the veal lung from the windpipe and gullet. Soak well, piercing several holes in the lung so that water can get into the cavity.
2. Fry the onion, cut surfaces down, in a pan until golden brown.
3. Fill a large pot with cold water, add lungs and heart and bring to boil. Add to the pot the root vegetables, peppercorns, allspice corns, bay leaf, thyme, salt and onion. Simmer until meat is tender.

4. Remove the lung after about 1 hour and rinse with cold water to cool. Leave the heart in the stock for at least another 30 minutes, until very tender, then remove.
5. Heat some of the stock in another saucepan and bring to boil.
6. Meanwhile, cut the lung and heart finely, removing any cartilage.
7. Heat some butter in a casserole dish. Sprinkle in the flour and sauté until light brown. Add the finely chopped innards seasoning: capers, onion, anchovy fillet, garlic, lemon rind, and parsley.
8. Let draw on low heat for a few minutes. Add the reduced stock, stir well and cook for 15-20 minutes until thick.
9. Add the innards and season with salt, pepper, vinegar, sugar, marjoram and mustard. As soon as the ragout is thick, stir in the sour cream and cream. Simmer for another 5-10 minutes.
10. Add lemon juice to taste and serve with a few drops of hot goulash juice and serve with bread dumplings.

Kärntner Kasnudeln, Austrian Pierogi

Yield: 4 servings

Ingredients:

300g coarse-grained flour
1 egg
A dash of oil
A pinch of salt
Egg white for coating
150g brown butter
Filling:
150g peeled potatoes
300g low fat quark
2 tbsps diced onion
1 egg, as required
2 tbsps mixed, finely-chopped herbs
3 tbsps sour cream, as required
Butter to sweat the onions
Salt

Directions:

1. To make the dough, make a pile of flour on the work surface, create a hollow in the middle and beat the egg into it. Salt the mix slightly.
2. Work in a little oil and sufficient water to produce a smooth, workable dough. Form into a ball, cover with film and leave to rest for 30–45 minutes.
3. Meanwhile cook the potatoes until soft, allow to cool briefly and press or sieve through a potato press.
4. Sweat the onions in butter, add the herbs, season with salt and remove from the heat. Mix all the ingredients together and work into a malleable paste filling. If necessary, loosen the mix with soured cream.
5. Roll out the dough on a floured work surface until it is the thickness of the back of a knife. Cut out disks of approximately 3 inch diameter using an upturned glass or circular cutter.
6. Shape small balls of the paste filling and place these on the dough circles, or use a spoon to apply the filling.

7. Coat the edges of the dough with the beaten egg white, fold the dough together and press firmly. Press the edges between the fingers to form grooves and set down on a floured board.
8. Heat up a generous quantity of salted water in a large pan. Place the pierogi into the water and, depending on size, leave to simmer gently for 10–12 minutes.
9. Remove carefully and arrange on preheated plates. Cover generously with foamed brown butter and serve. Serve with a refreshing green salad.

Käsespätzle

Yield: 2 servings

Ingredients:

250g flour
5 eggs + 1 egg yolk
3 tbsps water
30g butter
200g Gruyere cheese, grated
Salt
Onions:
75g butter
2 mid-sized onions cut in rings

Directions:

1. Start with combining flour, eggs and a good-sized pinch of salt. Blend well and add water if necessary, spoon by spoon.
2. The dough should not be runny, but soft enough to gradually follow gravitation. Then set aside and allow the dough to rest for 20 to 30 minutes.
3. Meanwhile heat the butter in a frying pan over low to medium heat, add onions, and let them slowly gain a golden brown colour. Don't let them get too dark, as they tend to become bitter. Drain on a paper towel and then set aside.
4. Bring a large pot of water briefly to a boil, add a pinch of salt and then reduce heat. The water should simmer throughout the whole process. You can either cut and shape the spätzle by hand or use a spätzle maker or a colander which makes things easier.
5. Cook the spätzle for about 2-3 minutes until they float back to the surface, then remove them.
6. When done, drain the water, melt 1-2 tbsp of butter and return the spätzle to the pot. Shake the pot a few times to evenly distribute the butter, then add the grated cheese and mix well.
7. Now simply add the browned onions and chopped chives on top and serve.

Pork Pot Roast

Yield: 6 servings

Ingredients:

3 carrots
250g celeriac
1 leek
500g each lean pork neck and belly fillet
½ bulb of fresh garlic
3 stems of thyme
4-5 stems of parsley
750g potatoes
1 stick of horseradish
1 apple
2 tsp lemon juice
1 tbsp clarified butter
Caraway seed
Juniper berries and peppercorns
Salt, pepper, sugar

Directions:

1. Wash the vegetables. Finely cut up 2 carrots, half the celeriac and half the leek. Cook in about 2 litres of water. Wash the meat.
2. Add seasoning, garlic and herbs to the vegetables, cover and simmer for about 1.5 hours.
3. Peel the potatoes, wash and cut into quarters. Cook in salt water for about 20 minutes. Sieve about 1 litre of bouillon, heat and reduce to about half.
4. Peel the apple and horseradish and grate finely. Mix with the lemon juice. Add salt, pepper and sugar to taste.
5. Cut the remaining vegetables into fine slices. Cover and cook in the bouillon for 5-7 minutes.
6. Drain the potatoes. Quickly sauté in hot clarified butter. Season with salt and caraway.
7. Cut the meat into thin strips. Serve with the sliced vegetables, stock, caraway potatoes and grated apple and horseradish.

Roast Beef

Yield: 4 servings

Ingredients:

4 slices roast beef or beef loin
6 shallots
1 small carrot
½ root parsley
1 small turnip
1 small piece of celery heart
1 tsp of chopped capers
50g bacon cubes
4 tbsps soured cream
1 tbsp flour for the sauce
400 ml beef stock
Grated lemon rind
Flour for coating
Salt, pepper
Chopped parsley

Directions:

1. Cut the roast beef several times around the edge and beat it gently. Season on both sides with salt and pepper, and coat one side in flour. Cut the shallots into fine strips.
2. Heat some fat in a pan, place the meat in with the floured side facing down and fry off briefly on a high heat. Turn the meat, remove it again after 2 minutes and place in a greased roasting dish with a lid.
3. Lightly brown the shallots in the same pan, adding some more butter as needed. Pour in some beef stock or water, bring to the boil and pour over the slices of beef.
4. Steam the meat over a low heat on the cooker or in a pre-heated oven at 180 °C for 60–90 minutes until soft, turning occasionally and topping up with liquid as required.
5. Meanwhile, slice the cleaned root vegetables into very fine strips and fry with the bacon in some hot fat. Add just a dash of beef stock and steam the vegetables until al dente.
6. Take the meat out of the dish. Mix the flour with the soured cream until smooth, pour into the juice and flavour with capers and grated lemon rind. Allow to boil off.
7. Put the meat back into the dish again briefly. Arrange and garnish with the sliced root vegetables. Sprinkle with parsley before serving.
8. Serve with pasta or fried potatoes.

Selchfleisch, Smoked Pork with Pea

Yield: 4 servings

Ingredients:

Smoked pork butt
⅓ cup diced bacon (3 slices)
½ cup finely chopped onions
3½ cups chicken stock, fresh or canned
1 pound dried green split peas, thoroughly washed and drained
2 medium-sized potatoes, peeled and diced (about 1½ cups)
½ teaspoon salt
½ cup heavy cream
Freshly ground black pepper

Directions:

1. Using a 4l saucepan or soup kettle, cover the pork butt with water and bring it to a boil. Reduce the heat to low, cover the pan partially, and simmer for about 1½ hours, or until the pork shows no resistance when pierced with the tip of a sharp knife.
2. In a heavy 2l saucepan over medium heat, cook the diced bacon until it has rendered most of its fat and is lightly browned. Remove the bacon with a slotted spoon and set it aside.
3. Add the onions to the fat remaining in the pan and, stirring occasionally, cook them for 6 to 8 minutes, or until they are lightly colored. Pour in the stock and then add the peas, the potatoes, the reserved bacon, salt and a few grindings of pepper.
4. Bring the stock to a boil before reducing the heat to its lowest point. Cover the pan tightly and simmer for 1½ hours, or until the peas and potatoes are soft enough to be easily mashed.
5. Then pour the entire contents of the pan into a fine sieve set over a large bowl, and puree the peas and potatoes by rubbing them through the sieve with the back of a large spoon.
6. Return the puree to the saucepan, add the cream, stir, and then turn the heat to its lowest point. Cover the saucepan and simmer for 4 or 5 minutes. Taste for seasoning.
7. Carve the pork butt into ¼ inch slices and arrange it on a platter. Serve the puree separately in a sauceboat.

Tafelspitz

Yield: 8 servings

Ingredients:

1,5kg beef topside
Beef bones
1 bunch of root vegetables
½ leek
1 large onion with skin
2 bay leaves
A few peppercorns
Salt

Directions:

1. Slice the unpeeled onion in half widthways and fry off the cut surfaces without fat until fairly well browned.
2. Put around 3 litres of water into a large saucepan. Add the root vegetables, leek, halves of onion, bay leaves and peppercorns and bring to the boil. Add the washed meat and bones and, depending on the type of meat, allow to cook until softened in gently simmering water, which will take around 2 ½ – 3 hours.
3. Meanwhile add more water as required and skim off any scum which comes to the surface.
4. Season well with salt, but only after a good 2 hours.
5. Once the meat has and softened, remove it from the pan and keep it warm in some of the liquid from the soup. Season the remainder of the soup again with salt to taste, and strain it, if preferred.
6. Slice the boiled beef by carving across the direction of the meat tissue and arrange as preferred on preheated plates. Serve with roast potatoes, a bread and horseradish mix, green beans in a dill sauce, or creamed spinach and chive sauce.

Tiroler Gröstl

Yield: 6 servings

Ingredients:

1½ tbsp corn, sunflower or veg. oil
400g smoked bacon lardons
1 onion, cut into chunks
500g cooked potatoes, cut into small chunks
1 tsp caraway seeds
1½ tsp sweet paprika
Small handful of parsley, roughly chopped

Directions:

1. Heat the oil in a large frying pan, then fry the bacon and onion together for 10 minutes until the bacon is golden.
2. Lift out of the pan onto a plate, before adding the potatoes and frying for 10 minutes more until golden.
3. Tip in the caraway and paprika, season well, and then fry for another minute, stirring to release their fragrance.
4. Return the bacon and onion, taste for seasoning, then add the parsley.
5. Serve hot and with a fried egg on top.

Viennese Char

Yield: 4 servings

Ingredients:

4 prepared whole char
Lemon juice
Flour for coating
200g butter
Freshly chopped parsley or tarragon
Salt
Pepper

Directions:

1. Wash the fish in cold water and pat dry using kitchen towel. Season the stomach cavity with salt and pepper. Season the outside of the char generously with salt and coat both sides in flour.
2. In a large pan (or ideally in 2 fish pans), slowly melt around half the butter (not allowing it to brown too much) and fry the char on both sides, depending on their size, for a total of 12-18 minutes until crispy and golden brown.
3. Carefully lift the char from the pan, arrange on preheated plates and keep warm by covering up with foil, or by placing in a pre-heated oven on low setting.
4. Now pour off any excess frying fat from the pan, introduce the rest of the butter and allow to bubble up, before adding a generous squeeze of lemon juice. Add salt and allow to bubble up again.
5. Drizzle over the char on the plates and then scatter on the freshly chopped parsley.
6. Serve with potatoes coated with butter or parsley, accompanied by a seasonal salad.

Viennese Goulash

Yield: 8 servings

Ingredients:

2l water
1,5kg beef shank
1,25kg onions
150g dripping or oil
2 tbsps tomato paste
4 tbsps paprika powder, sweet
2 cloves of garlic
A little lemon rind, grated
Apple vinegar
2 juniper berries, pressed
Pinch of marjoram
Pinch of ground caraway seeds
Pinch of sugar
Ground pepper
2 tbsps flour
Salt

Directions:

1. Slice onions. Cut the meat into bite sized cubes.
2. Heat the dripping in a large pot and fry the onions until golden brown. Add juniper berries, marjoram, caraway seeds, sugar, pepper and salt and briefly sauté.
3. Stir in paprika powder, tomato paste, garlic and lemon rind and quickly add vinegar and 1 litre of water. Bring to boil then and add cubed meat and let stew for about 2 1/2 hours. Stir repeatedly and add water if necessary.
4. When the meat is almost done, stir well and add the rest of the water.
5. Let cook for a while longer then add salt to taste.
6. Mix the flour with a bit of water, stir and add to the goulash to bind.
7. Serve with fresh bread or baked potatoes.

Wiener Schnitzel

Yield: 4 servings

Ingredients:

4 veal schnitzel
2 eggs
100g coarse-ground flour
100g breadcrumbs
Clarified butter
Slices of lemon, to garnish
Salt, pepper

Directions:

1. Lay out the schnitzel, remove any skin and beat until thin. Season on both sides with salt and pepper.
2. Place flour and breadcrumbs into separate flat plates, beat the eggs together on a further plate using a fork.
3. Coat each schnitzel firstly on both sides in flour, then draw through the beaten eggs, ensuring that no part of the schnitzel remains dry. Lastly, coat in the breadcrumbs and carefully press down the crumbs using the reverse side of the fork.
4. In a large pan, melt sufficient clarified butter for the schnitzel to be able to swim freely in the oil.
5. Only place the Schnitzel in the pan when the fat is so hot that it hisses and bubbles up if some breadcrumbs or a small piece of butter is introduced to it.
6. Depending on the thickness and the type of meat, fry for between 2 minutes and 4 minutes until golden brown. Turn using a spatula and fry on the other side until similarly golden brown.
7. Serve golden fries schnitzels with potatoes and tartar sauce.

Desserts

Kaiserschmarrn

Apfelstrudel

Ingredients:

Puff pastry
1,5kg apples
100g sugar
4 tbsps raisins
Rum
Lemon juice
Cinnamon
Powdered cloves
Icing sugar for dusting
Plenty of melted butter
100g breadcrumbs
3 tbsp butter
3 tbsp grated hazelnuts

Directions:

1. Steep the raisins in the rum and leave to soak.
2. To prepare the nutty breadcrumbs, heat the butter in a pan until it bubbles up. Add the breadcrumbs and fry slowly over a moderate heat until golden brown. Towards the end, stir in the grated nuts, cook through quickly and remove from the heat.
3. Peel the apples, cut into slices and quickly sprinkle with lemon juice. Then, depending on the acidity of the apples, add a suitable amount of sugar and powdered cloves, and mix in a generous pinch of cinnamon.
4. Pre-heat the oven to 180°C and grease a suitable baking tin with butter.
5. Distribute the nutty breadcrumbs over around half of the dough. Scatter the apples and raisins over it.
6. Coat the remaining surface of the dough generously with melted butter, fold in the edges at the sides and roll up the strudel. Seal the ends well and lift the strudel into the baking tin using the baking paper.
7. Depending on the dough, coat with melted butter and bake for 30 minutes until golden brown.
8. Remove the finished strudel, leave to cool down and sprinkle with icing sugar.

Easter Cake

Ingredients:

500g flour
250ml milk
40g yeast
2 eggs
90g sugar
120g butter
Pinch of salt
Filling:
50g butter
100g raisins
100g sugar
1 tbsp cinnamon
100g finely ground nuts

Directions:

1. First, mix the flour with the yeast and add a bit of milk and sugar until you get a smooth mixture. Cover it with a piece of cloth and let it rest in a warm place for half an hour.
2. Then add the rest of the milk and the sugar, the eggs, the butter and a pinch of salt, and work it into a smooth dough. Let it rest again, this time for 10 minutes. Then roll out the dough so that it is roughly as thick as your thumb.
3. For the filling, melt the butter and spread it on the dough. Mix the sugar with the cinnamon and sprinkle the dough. Then add the raisins and, if you like, the nuts.
4. After that, roll the dough up tightly and put it into a greased cake pan. Again, let it rest for 20 minutes.
5. Finally, sprinkle little bits of butter on the cake. Then put it in the oven for 50 - 60 minutes at about 180°C.
6. When it is done, take it out of the oven and let it cool.
7. Only turn the cake out of the pan when it is completely cold to avoid it breaking

Emperor's Gugelhupf

To perform this recipe get gugelhupf mold.

Ingredients:

210g fine cake flour
170g granulated sugar
210g butter
5 eggs
50g raisins soaked in rum
80g chopped walnuts
1 packet vanilla sugar
1tsp baking powder
Peel from half an unsprayed lemon
Melted butter for the mould
Almond flakes

Directions:

1. Grease the Gugelhupf mould with butter. Scatter the almond flakes into the mould.
2. Preheat the oven to around 170°C.
3. Cream the room-temperature butter with two-thirds of the granulated sugar and vanilla sugar. Gradually stir in the egg yolks. Flavour with grated lemon peel.
4. Beat the egg whites with a pinch of salt and the remaining granulated sugar to form stiff peaks.
5. Mix the flour with the baking powder and fold into the egg yolk mix, alternating with the whites. Dust the well-drained raisins lightly with flour and stir in together with the walnuts.
6. Pour into the prepared mould and bake for 45 – 50 minutes until golden brown. Allow to cool briefly, and then turn out. Dust with icing sugar.
7. Cut the Gugelhupf into slices and garnish to taste with sweetened whipped cream.

Germknödel

Ingredients:

500g strong white flour
7g instant, dried yeast
1 tsp salt
65 g sugar
70 g butter, melted
250g whole milk, warmed
1 egg yolk
1 egg
1 lemon, zest
1/2 tsp vanilla extract
Filling:
300g Powidl
1 tbsp rum
Serving:
150g poppy seeds, ground
Icing sugar
Vanilla sauce

Directions:

1. Combine all dumpling ingredients and knead for about 10 minutes. You should have a soft, smooth, workable dough – not too sticky and not too dry.
2. Place the dough in a plastic bowl, cover and leave to rise somewhere warm for an hour or two until it has doubled in size. How quickly the rise happens depends on the temperature in the room, so be patient in case it takes a little longer.
3. In a small bowl, mix Powidl and rum.
4. Lightly flour a clean work surface and turn out the dough.
5. Punch down the dough, form the dough into a sausage shape and divide into 10 pieces with your dough scraper.
6. Flatten each piece with your hand.
7. Place a teaspoon of Powidl mixture into the centre of the flat round dough piece.
8. Bring up the sides of the dough around the plum jam and seal well by pinching the edges.
9. Place each dumpling onto the floured work surface or baking sheet, cover with a dish towel and leave to prove for about 30 minutes to 1 hour. The Germknödel should have visibly risen before you continue.
10. Prepare the vanilla sauce while you wait.

11. Bring a large pan of water to the boil and use a steamer (I use a bamboo steamer) lined with baking paper to steam the dumplings for 15 minutes. I can fit four dumplings into my steamer at a time. Make sure you cover the steamer with a lid.
12. If you don't have a steamer, you can use a cotton dish towel which you put over the pan. Secure it with twine and make sure the cloth isn't exposed to the heat source. Place the dumplings onto the cloth and cover with a second pot.
13. Serve and enjoy straight away. Pour over hot vanilla sauce and sprinkle with a mix of ground poppy seeds and icing sugar.

Chocolate Gugelhupf

To perform this recipe get gugelhupf mold.

Ingredients:

5 eggs
150g icing sugar
180g butter
100g grated hazelnuts
100g cooking chocolate
2 tbsps cocoa powder
100g plain flour
1 tsp baking powder
Pinch of salt
Butter for the mould
Redcurrant jam
Cracknel or roughly chopped nuts
Glaze:
130g cooking chocolate
130g butter
1 tbsp of coconut fat

Directions:

1. Beat the egg yolks with the icing sugar, add the butter and cream.
2. Preheat oven to 180°C and grease the Gugelhupf mold with melted butter.
3. Whip up the egg whites with a small pinch of salt and the granulated sugar to stiff peaks. Melt the chocolate coating in a bain-marie.
4. Mix the flour with the baking powder and add to the egg yolk mix together with grated nuts, cocoa powder and melted chocolate. Carefully fold in the egg whites.
5. Pour the mixture into the mold and bake 50 – 55 minutes.
6. Cool slightly, and tip out.
7. Cover the lukewarm Gugelhupf with the redcurrant jam and leave to cool.
8. Melt the chocolate in a bain-marie together with butter and coconut fat and stir. Continue stirring until it has cooled.
9. Cover the Gugelhupf with the glaze and sprinkle with cracknel or chopped nuts.

Kaiserschmarrn

Ingredients:

6 eggs
400 ml milk
200 g finely ground flour
3 tbsps crystal sugar, for the topping
2 tbsps raisins
1 packet vanilla sugar
A dash of rum
A pinch of salt
50g butter for frying
1 tablespoon of butter shavings and crystal sugar, for caramelising
Icing sugar and cinnamon for dusting
Some grated lemon rind

Directions:

1. Place the raisins in a bowl, mix with the rum and leave to stand for approx. 15 minutes.
2. Separate the eggs and place the yolks in a mixing bowl. Pour in the milk, flavour with some grated lemon rind and vanilla sugar, and add the flour. Mix to form a smooth dough.
3. Beat the egg whites with the crystal sugar and a small pinch of salt until it forms a firm peak, and fold into the dough mix.
4. Preheat the oven to 180 °C.
5. Let the butter melt and bubble up in one large, or two small heatproof dishes.
6. Pour in the mixture and after 1–2 minutes scatter the soaked raisins over the top. Cook the underside until light brown, turn over using a spatula and bake for 6–8 minutes in the pre-heated oven until golden brown.
7. Tear the 'Schmarren' into small pieces, using two forks. Scatter the butter shavings over the top, sprinkle with some crystal sugar, and caramelise under the grill at a high heat.
8. Remove from the grill and arrange on preheated plates. Dust with icing sugar and cinnamon.
9. Serve with baked plums, a berry ragout or fruit compote.

Linzer Torte

Ingredients:

250g butter
250g flour
125g icing sugar
150g ground hazelnuts (or almonds)
2 tbsps bread crumbs
1 egg
1 egg yolk
Generous quantity of cinnamon powder
A pinch of ground cloves
A pinch of salt
Grated lemon rind or lemon juice
Wafers for layering, to taste
Egg for coating
Redcurrant jam for coating
Butter for the mould
Flaked almonds, to taste

Directions:

1. Create a pile of flour on the work surface, slice the butter into cubes and rub between the fingers into the flour to create a light crumb. Flavour with the cinnamon, a pinch of ground cloves and a little salt, together with the lemon rind or lemon juice and ground nuts.
2. Work quickly to form a smooth short pastry, shape into a ball, cover with film and leave to rest in a cool place for approx. 30 minutes.
3. Pre-heat the oven to 180 °C. Grease a suitably sized spring form cake tin and then dust with the breadcrumbs to prevent the dough from sticking.
4. Now press a little over half of the dough onto the base of the tin, using the knuckles of the fingers. Shape the remaining dough into several small rolls (for the lattice) and one thicker roll (for the edge). If you like, cover the pastry base with wafers, and then coat with smoothly stirred jam, leaving about 1/2 inch all round for the edge. Place the thicker roll into the tin as an edging, and press down gently. Use the thinner rolls to create a lattice. Sprinkle with flaked almonds to taste.
5. Coat the dough with the beaten egg and bake in the pre-heated oven for 50–60 minutes.
6. Take out the tart, leave to cool, and ideally leave to stand for a day, wrapped in film. Dust with icing sugar.

Palatschinken

Ingredients:

1 cup all-purpose flour
1 pinch of salt
2 tbsps sugar
240ml milk
2 large eggs

Directions:

1. Whisk the flour, milk, sugar, and salt together until smooth, then whisk in the eggs.
2. Heat 2 tablespoons of oil in a pan over medium-high heat and start the first pancake by pouring in roughly 4 tablespoons of batter.
3. The pan floor should be covered thinly but completely. Allow to brown slightly, turn, and brown on the other side. Remove and continue making the individual pancakes, stacking them as they are ready.
4. Keep warm on a covered plate. Add 2 tablespoons of oil for each pancake.
5. Serve spread with jam and rolled.

Sachertorte

Ingredients:

7 egg yolks
150g softened butter
125g icing sugar
200g dark chocolate
1 packet vanilla sugar
7 egg whites
125g crystal sugar
150g flour
200g apricot jam, for spreading
Rum, if desired
Whipped cream to garnish
Butter and flour for the mould
A pinch of salt
Glaze:
200g dark chocolate coating or cooking chocolate
250g sugar
170ml water

Directions:

1. Melt the chocolate slowly (ideally in a bain-marie). Meanwhile, mix the butter with the icing sugar and vanilla sugar until creamed. Gradually stir in the egg yolks.
2. Pre-heat the oven to 180 °C. Grease a cake tin with butter and sprinkle with flour.
3. Whip up the egg whites with a pinch of salt, add the crystal sugar and beat to a stiff peak. Stir the melted chocolate into the paste with the egg yolks and fold in the whipped egg whites alternately with the flour.
4. Fill the dough into the tin and bake for around 1 hour.
5. Remove the cake and leave to cool off.
6. If the apricot jam is too solid, heat it briefly and stir until smooth, before flavouring with a shot of rum.
7. Cut the cake in half crosswise. Cover the base with jam, set the other half on top, and coat the upper surface and around the edges with apricot jam.

8. For the glaze, break the chocolate into small pieces. Heat up the water with the sugar for a few minutes. Pour into a bowl and leave to cool down until just warm to the taste. Add the chocolate and dissolve in the sugar solution.
9. Pour the glaze quickly over the cake and immediately spread it out and smooth it over the surface, using a palate knife or other broad-bladed knife.
10. Leave the cake to dry at room temperature.

Salzburger Nockerl

Ingredients:

150ml milk
½ vanilla pod
Freshly squeezed lemon juice
7 egg whites
Pinch of salt
80g sugar
4 egg yolks
Rind from 1 lemon
10g grated vanilla sugar
2 tsp flour
1 tsp cornstarch
Icing sugar for dusting
Butter for greasing

Directions:

1. Heat the milk with the cut-open vanilla pod and lemon juice. Remove from the stove and leave to sit. Remove the pod. Smear an oval-shaped, ovenproof form with butter and pour in enough vanilla milk to cover the bottom.
2. With a hand mixer, mix the cooled egg whites with a pinch of salt and a third of the sugar until very stiff. Slowly add the rest of the sugar and continue to beat until the mixture is thick and creamy.
3. Preheat the oven to 220°C. Add the egg yolks, lemon rind, vanilla sugar, flour, and cornstarch to the egg white mixture and fold three or four times with a whisk.
4. Make 4 pyramid-shaped nockerl, placing them next to each other in the baking tray. Bake for 10-12 minutes until light, golden brown.
5. Dust with icing sugar and serve quickly so that the Nockerl don't collapse.

Wachauer Marillenknödel, Apricot Dumplings

Ingredients:

300g low-fat quark
200g flour
60g butter, at room temperature
1 packet vanilla sugar
1 egg
A pinch of salt
10 small apricots
10 sugar cubes
Topping:
100g breadcrumbs
100g butter
Cinnamon powder
Icing sugar

Directions:

1. Mix the softened butter with the vanilla sugar and a small pinch of salt until creamed through. Stir in the egg with the quark and flour and work into a malleable dough. Form into a ball, wrap in film and leave in a cool place to rest for approx. 30 minutes.
2. Remove the stones from the apricots and place a sugar cube in their place.
3. On a floured work surface shape the dough into a roll of approx. 2 inch thickness. Cut off slices and gently press these flat between the hands.
4. Place the apricot into the dough, press the dough around it and seal well. Apply some flour to the hands, form dumplings and place on a similarly-floured board.
5. Bring a generous amount of slightly-salted water to the boil in a large saucepan. Turn down the heat, place the apricot dumplings in the water and allow to simmer gently for 10–13 minutes. Stir carefully from time to time to prevent the dumplings from sticking to one another.
6. For the garnish, melt the butter in a pan. Add the breadcrumbs, flavour with cinnamon and fry until golden yellow in colour. Towards the end, add a generous quantity of sugar.
7. Carefully remove the cooked dumplings and roll in the prepared sugared bread crumbs.
8. Arrange and dust with icing sugar.

Side Dishes

Potato Dumplings

Basic scalloped potatoes

Ingredients:

6 large potatoes
2 large onions
2 cups of cream
Marjoram
Olive oil
Salt

Directions:

1. Slice peeled potatoes and place them in baking pan.
2. Add salt, marjoram and grated onion. Finally pour with cream.
3. Bake it for 25 minutes at 200°C.

Mashed potatoes

Ingredients:

6 large potatoes
250ml milk (or sour cream)
25g butter
Crushed cumin
Salt
Optionally: fried diced bacon

Directions:

4. Boil peeled diced potatoes for 30 minutes. Meanwhile heat up the milk.
5. Strain the water, add butter and mash potatoes while pouring milk.
6. You can add fried diced bacon.

Bread dumplings

Ingredients:

500g flour
2 buns
25g yeast
300ml milk
1 tablespoon of sugar
Salt

Directions:

1. Mix flour, finely diced buns and milk. Add yeast, salt, sugar and make dough. Leave it to rest for 45 minutes.
2. Split dough into two pieces and shape them in cylinders.
3. Boil them in salt water for 17 minutes. Serve sliced.

Potato dumplings

Ingredients:

800g potatoes
200g flour
2 eggs
100g semolina
2 tablespoons of vinegar
Salt

Ingredients:

1. Cook potatoes. Grate them without peel.
2. Mix with flour, semolina, salt, egg and vinegar. Make dough. Split it in four pieces and shape into cylinders.
3. Boil for 20 minutes. Serve sliced.

Volume Conversion

Customary Quantity	Metric Equivalent
1 teaspoon	5 ml
1 tablespoon	15ml
1/8 cup	30 ml
1/4 cup	60 ml
1/3 cup	80 ml
1/2 cup	120 ml
2/3 cup	160 ml
3/4 cup	180 ml
1 cup	240 ml
1 1/2 cups	360 ml
2 cups	480 ml
3 cups	720 ml
4 cups	960 ml

Weights of Common Ingredients

Ingredient	1 cup	1/2 cup	2 Tbs
Flour	120 g	70 g	15 g
Sugar	200 g	100 g	25 g
Rice	190 g	100 g	24 g
Macaroni	140 g	70 g	17 g
Butter	240 g	120 g	30 g
Chopped Nuts	150 g	75 g	20 g
Bread Crumbs	150 g	75 g	20 g
Grated Cheese	90 g	45 g	11 g

Temperature Conversion

Fahrenheit	Celsius
250	120
275	140
300	150
325	160
c350	180
375	190
400	200
425	220
450	203

Length Conversion

Inch	cm
0,125	0,32
0,25	0,63
0,5	1,27
1	2,54
2	5,08
5	12,7

Thank you, my reader, for investing time and money to read this book!

The stores all full of many books dedicated to cooking either collecting and sharing recipes or presenting new ones. I sincerely thank you for choosing this very book and reading it to its very end.

I hope you have enjoyed this book as much as possible and that you have learnt something new and interesting. If you have enjoyed this book, please take a few minutes to write a review summarizing your thoughts and opinion on this book.

If you are interested in other paperback books of mine check out my official amazon author's profile:

www.amazon.com/author/prochazkacook

Thanks for buying this books and have best of luck.

Sincerely,

Lukas Prochazka

Learn more about European cuisines

If you are interested in other European countries you should consider checking out the other European cookbooks.

German, an unrepeatable neighbour of Czechia, is a country with a huge national heritage including the cuisine. German cuisine greatly influenced the cuisine of the United States, especially the most popular food, hamburger.

German Eintopf is most of times regarded as a cooking joke, but it can be tasty. Learn more about this iconic German meal

Czech cuisine is regarded as one of the best cuisine by the experts yet it gets little attention. Learn how to make genuine Czech meals.

If you want to learn more about Czech pubs and the meal served in those, check out the Czech Pub Food cookbook.

Poland is an eastern country with huge national heritage proven. Even though Poland has been through tough history its time-proven culture stands unharmed. Polish cuisine is full of rich flavours. Learn how to make genuine Polish meals.

Printed in Great Britain
by Amazon

53857922R00034